STEER
THE
WHEEL

…to keep your organization rolling smoothly.

Steer the Wheel
...to keep your organization rolling smoothly.
Copyright © 2008 by Jeffrey L. Corkran.

Although the author and publisher have made every effort to ensure the accuracy and completeness of information contained in this book, including attribution of quotes, we assume no responsibility for errors, inaccuracies, omissions, or any inconsistencies herein. Any slights of people ore organizations are unintentional.

First printing 2008

ATTENTION CORPORATIONS AND PROFESSIONAL ORGANIZATIONS:
Quantity discounts are available on bulk purchases of this book for educational, training, or gift purposes.

For information, please contact C2C Training and Consulting, 108 Amanda Court, Radcliff, KY 40160. 270-317-3090.

Library of Congress Cataloging-In-Publication Data

Corkran, Jeffrey L.
      Steer the Wheel: ...to keep your organization rolling smoothly/by Jeffrey L. Corkran. 1st ed.

Includes bibliographical references.

      ISBN: 978-1438248066
      1. Leadership 2. Business and Economics
      3. Self-help I. Title

Book edited by MarJean Corkran and Don K. Corkran
Cover Design by Dennis Estanislao, Forward Animation

Contents

Acknowledgments   v

Preface   ix

Chapter One – Defining Leadership   1

Chapter Two – The Wheel   17

Chapter Three – The Wheel and the Absent Leader   47

Chapter Four – The Wheel Compared to other   61
Leadership Models

Chapter Five – The Wheel and Your Boss   73

Chapter Six – The Wheel and the New leader –   81
Starting Right

Chapter Seven – Leadership Lessons I've Learned   93

Bibliography   112

Contact Information   112

Acknowledgments

This book, as any other such project, required support and encouragement from many other people. I suppose some authors can sit down and write, edit, and publish their manuscripts but that is not the case here. This one required a lot of support from my family and friends.

Without doubt, the biggest load of appreciation goes to Dee, my wonderful wife, who never failed to encourage and support my decision to write this. She remains absolutely my biggest fan and heartiest encourager, without whom I would seldom accomplish anything worthwhile. Dee, I love you dearly and thank you profusely for all you do to support me daily.

Thanks also to all my children, who encouraged me to complete the project and never questioned why I would want to do such a thing. Never once did any of them suggest I could not or would not succeed, but always believed in me. So, thanks to all of you – Stephanie, Paul, Josh, and Rachael – for having confidence in me.

Thanks to Dennis Estanislao, son-in-law #2, of Forward Animation for designing the book cover, as well as for all the work on the web site. Your talent continues to amaze me.

Having tried for a while to get someone actually to read my draft manuscript, thanks to my niece, MarJean Corkran, for finally reading it and giving me some editing help in making it coherent. MarJean is an English instructor at a college in Alabama and I am not quite sure why I didn't think of her in the first place! Then after seeing the first proof copy in print, my brother, Don Corkran – also a retired soldier – gave me more help with the editing and layout. (Of course, as two old soldiers, I'm sure we drove our parents slightly nuts over the years, but all our talks about effective leadership certainly helped me develop. Thanks for those talks, too, Don.)

Some colleagues are special. To my old friends and colleagues Lindon Coffee and Dr. Alonzo Johnson, thanks for helping me get the initial idea for this book and for helping convince me I could do it. I will always remember our talks and hope to continue our friendship and professional association.

Finally, thanks to <u>all</u> the leaders who have helped me learn and develop over the years.

Preface

Leadership is both an art and a science. The *science* of leadership involves a set of skills that we can learn and practice. Generally, the same skills and techniques work effectively the majority of the time with the majority of people. Learning and applying these skills and techniques enables individuals to become effective leaders. This is a scientific approach – applying the same factors in given situations will produce predictable results. In this case, those results are effective leadership and accomplishment of goals and objectives. Please note that the key here is <u>effective</u> leadership. Placing someone in a position of authority establishes that person as a leader but only applying the appropriate practices can make that same individual an *effective* leader. Merely having the position makes the person an authority figure – not an effective leader.

The *art* of leadership is making all the tools, techniques, and practices work at appropriate times and in appropriate situations. Simply put, the techniques clearly don't always work the same. People are fickle, emotional, unpredictable, and inconsistent. If we were totally predictable, anyone could be an effective leader. Unfortunately, that is not the case. We – people – don't always respond to situations in the same way. Vast differences exist between people and each of us shows significant differences in various circumstances. The artistic leader knows when to use what technique, method, or motivator for a specific individual in a specific situation. Ken Blanchard and Paul Hersey made the idea of situational leadership quite well known in the late 1960s, but many leaders still try to use a one-size-fits-all philosophy in 2007.

The point of this book is to present a model that makes sense to leaders at all levels of all types of organizations. It is a reminder of some basic tenets of leadership, rather than a panacea for all the woes of leadership we face. A return to basics often helps us be more effective. Good leadership has always been good leadership and will remain that way. The factors that differentiate between effective and ineffective leadership now are the same as they were thousands of years ago. So this book won't present leadership techniques or philosophies that are brand new or that you have never heard before. What it will do is talk about leadership and organizations in a way that hopefully will help some readers turn on a light and understand, finally, how leadership works.

My real motivator for writing this book is that I am truly passionate about leadership. That passion comes from many years of having seen excellent leaders at all levels of many types of organizations and having observed very poor, ineffective leaders in those same organizations. In my opinion, leadership is a noble undertaking, regardless of the organization's purpose or structure. Whether in a major corporation, military unit, small business, local government, non-profit organization, or any other structure, leadership is critical in today's world. Helping others succeed while accomplishing the organization's mission at the same time is no small matter and is the ultimate goal of leadership.

If this book helps *anyone* become a better leader, I have accomplished what I set out to do.

Jeff Corkran

Chapter One
Defining Leadership

All of us know a great leader when we see one. The signs are unmistakable, the results indisputable, the evidence clear. Do we all recognize the same signs and signals of great leadership? Or do we spend most of our lives debating and arguing with each other about what does or does not constitute good leadership? For example, most Americans think of Abraham Lincoln and George Washington as great Presidents – outstanding leaders for their times who rose to the occasion to make our country strong. Douglas MacArthur, George S. Patton, Erwin Rommel, Robert E. Lee, and many others are widely regarded as extremely capable, effective military leaders of the past. More recently, you can pick a military leader of conflicts in the Middle East or Afghanistan as an example of an effective leader. We all have favorite presidents, senators, or other politicians whom we regard as leaders best suited to guide our country. Those choices often have little to do with the individual's leadership ability. We consider Bill Gates, Warren Buffett, Jack Welch, and hundreds more effective, even amazing leaders of business. But if we study the history, Washington and Lincoln had opponents, competitors, and even enemies. In both these cases, other men felt they were more capable and suitable than the men whose names we remember today.

3

So leadership, its definition, the factors that make it effective, or inspired, or great are not quite as clear as we might believe. Ask 1,000 people what leadership is, get 1,000 answers. Ask those same 1,000 people what *effective* leadership is and you will probably get something less than 1,000 answers, at least initially. Over time, specific themes of effective leadership have been discussed, debated, and written about extensively. In training leaders, I often ask them to think of a great leader they have known. International leaders, parents, sports team coaches, anyone is allowed because great leaders are everywhere. Without fail, many of the same ideas and concepts surface every time. Words such as courage, fair, good listener, consistent, caring, good communicator, and knowledgeable come to everyone's mind as we consider what makes people good, effective leaders. There are certainly differences between the ideas expressed by various groups of people, but many of the same ideas surface every time. Most of us recognize when our leaders are effective, but seldom do we stop to determine why. Those of us who subsequently accept positions of leadership even less frequently remember all those factors that made our leaders effective and apply them to our own leadership styles. We all remember the bad leaders/bosses we have had and swear we will not act that way when we are in charge, but reality is often quite different.

So just what is leadership? Is it setting the example, caring for people, always making the right decisions? Is it accomplishing goals regardless of how their accomplishment affects followers, making sure we achieve a good bottom line, pleasing the boss? Yes and no. It is all of those things and none of those things. "Leadership," in and of itself, is just getting others to do what we want them to do. Consequently, the term encompasses every kind of leader – from the most effective team builders to the most tyrannical dictators. Granted, when we think of leaders today, we are unlikely to think of tyrants or dictators, but they are leaders. And some totalitarian leaders have been quite effective throughout history. For our purposes, however, we are talking about modern effective leadership.

All right, so we're talking about effective leadership. What does that mean? Again, for purposes of discussion, *effective* leadership is getting others to do what we want, but getting them to do so productively, willingly, and relatively happily. "Happily?" Wait just a minute! Do I really mean that people need to be *happy* in accomplishing organizational

goals and objectives? Well, no, they don't <u>have</u> to be happy.
But they are sure more likely to accomplish what you want
them to do if they are happy about it and committed to doing
it. Quite simply, happy people – or at least people who are
relatively pleased about what they are doing – will perform at
a higher level.

We could argue that even the definition of effective
leadership is unclear. Effective according to whom? Most
people, even leaders, report to other leaders. Our leaders can
see us as effective in their eyes, while our followers see us
simultaneously with great contempt. So is *effective
leadership* just getting the job done or does it include the
willing, happy productivity we discussed in the preceding
paragraph? Yes. Both. Neither. Obviously, we can debate
the definition of effective leadership as long as we want,
without ever coming to complete agreement. For the
purposes of this work, *effective leadership* means both getting
organizational goals accomplished in an effective, timely
manner and keeping followers happy, involved, and willingly
productive.

Let's face it: the great majority of us have to work to
support our families and ourselves. The American people

accepted that long ago. America may be the land of milk and honey where dreams come true, but the milk and honey are not free. In fact, sometimes the dreams aren't even free. No, the average American has accepted the plight of having to work to achieve his or her goals and dreams. (I maintain that even those who do not have to work will engage in productive activities similar to work – volunteering with a charity, pursuing a productive hobby, or some other equivalent undertaking but that is beyond the scope of this discussion.) We don't mind having to work to reach our goals, but we do want respect and appreciation along the way. This gets us to what an effective leader provides an organization. The three main functions a leader provides are:

1. The vision and guidance to chart a course for the organization,
2. The tools and resources to get the job done, and
3. The environment to keep people happy.

Of course, these functions involve many separate attitudes and actions. Merely stating that they are important does not make us good leaders. However, keeping them in mind will help us stay focused as leaders, especially when organizational business has a tendency to overwhelm us. Let's talk about each of these three functions separately.

Vision

Leaders at all levels of organizations often get caught up in the moment and get so overwhelmed with the multitude and magnitude of everyday actions that they forget to lead. They think leading is handling everything and making all decisions. This is micromanaging, not leading. Of course, these leaders do need to be aware of what is going on in the organization, be flexible enough to travel to different parts of the organization and see situations for themselves, and understand when to step in and personally control specific situations. On a daily basis, however, subordinate leaders or other workers need to make many decisions. Allowing these people the freedom to make appropriate decisions not only frees the leader to focus on other issues, but also helps develop them as leaders, as well. A shared vision helps these subordinates know where their actions and decisions need to take the organization. Truly effective leaders share a clear vision with subordinates, allow them to make appropriate decisions (including a few bad ones), and inspire them to want to reach that vision.

Including others in the development of the vision helps in getting their support in reaching that vision. Leaders are responsible for the vision, but can seldom reach that vision alone. Inspiring others and getting them excited in reaching a vision are invaluable in gaining willing, enthusiastic followers. One way to get them excited is to involve them in the development of the vision.

Tools and Resources

Merely to state that subordinates need the tools to do what we need them to do is much too simple. "Must provide own tools" usually does not apply in organizations. Leaders must ensure that workers have what they need to succeed and to achieve organizational goals. Expecting them to do what we want them to do without providing tools and resources is expecting too much.

So what do they need? That certainly depends on the job they are being asked to do. *Tools* may include many items, including hammers, impact wrenches, computers, or whatever. As a leader, you need to know what these tools are and listen to subordinates who request items they need but do not have. Every job, every organization uses different tools.

More importantly, employees need *resources*. Many leaders make their mistakes in this area. Raw materials are obviously critical in production facilities. Policies and procedures, integral parts of the model described in the next chapter, let the employee know what to do and how to do it. Standardized work instructions ensure quality. All of these are resources. Quite often, the most forgotten resource that employees need is *information.* People want to know how they are performing – good and bad. They want to know what is going on and where the organization is heading. They want feedback on performance and input into upcoming changes in the organization. They want leaders to respect them as people, with the acknowledgment that there is life beyond the workplace. Finally, they want to be respected for what they do, what they know and what they contribute. Failure of a leader to meet these needs is just as devastating as failing to provide tools and raw materials.

<u>Happiness</u>

Must people really be happy at work or in an organization? Well, no. We can conduct the business of the organization regardless of the happiness of the people in it. Workers – people – who know where they are going, feel that what they are doing is worthwhile, and who truly believe in what they are doing and are happy about it will work hard to achieve the desired results. Simply put, *happy* people come to work more reliably, stay in the workplace longer, and work more productively while they are there. On the other end of the spectrum, unhappy people call in sick more frequently, bounce from job to job, and perform at minimum or mediocre levels.

The two leadership functions discussed above: vision and guidance, and providing tools and resources, are essential in ensuring happy workers. Providing a leadership climate in which people can be themselves, make honest mistakes, and develop professionally and personally completes the happiness equation. People want their leaders to recognize that they are more than just workers. They want leaders who acknowledge there is life beyond the workplace, that they have families and other interests, and that they may occasionally make mistakes. Finally, people want to feel that what they are doing is worthwhile, that it matters. This is a key ingredient to building and maintaining self-esteem. Happy people with good solid self-esteem are just more valuable to your organization. While quite simplistic, this statement is the essence of helping people stay happy at work, whether in a paid workplace or volunteer situation.

People also want to be involved in deciding where they and the organization are going. When challenged to help map out a strategy, vision, or new direction for an organization, people will work amazingly hard and will display incredible creativity. Even if they do not individually agree with the final decision, having input into the process helps people embrace new ideas and directions and go there happily. Of course, if none of their ideas are ever seriously considered, that happiness and willingness can rapidly fade. If properly challenged and inspired, they will develop amazingly creative ideas. Remember that these people make the organization work. They are the ones who deal with customers, manufacture products, and get all the work done. They're pretty smart at it, too.

A few years ago, I was consulting with a local plant of a major corporation in developing a strategic plan for their facility. In preparing for the actual planning sessions, I asked one of the major local leaders if they received a strategic plan from corporate headquarters. Of course, he replied that they did. The remainder of the conversation went something like this:

"Where is it?" I asked.

"Over there in the safe," he replied.

"How do your folks on the production floor know what it says?" I asked.

"Oh, we can't tell them that!" he said, with great animation.

"Why not? Who does the work? Who accomplishes the goals and objectives in that plan?" I asked further. This was getting very interesting.

Silence for a few moments.

"Jeff, the sheep don't have to know that the shepherd is taking them to greener pastures. They just have to trust the shepherd." Jack (the leader) was enjoying himself now.

"Yes, but what if the sheep knew where those pastures were and could go there by themselves because they had helped pick the pastures in the first place? Aren't there other things the shepherd could be doing in the mean time?" Two can enjoy this game.

Another short silence.

"Damn it, Jeff. I hate it when you're right," he finally conceded. I had achieved my goal for that round.

By the way, I got the consulting contract and the plant's strategic planning team, including union members, developed a great plan that helped them make wonderful progress over the next few years. (Jack was also opposed to including union members on the team.) Keeping people at all levels of the organization involved in the planning made them happier about achieving the goals and objectives contained in the plan. Having fellow workers involved on the planning team also let others in the plant know that this wasn't the latest "flavor of the week" from the management group, thus getting everyone committed to achieving the goals and objectives desired. Without getting into specifics, let me say that company is now the fourth largest of its kind *in the world*. They didn't get there by accident. They got there through effective leadership.

Application

As a leader, you are responsible for what happens in your organization, department, section, or division. Keep in mind that leaders at all levels are still leaders. Don't blame others for what happens in your world – <u>you</u> are the responsible party. Too often, we tend to blame our bosses or outside influences, instead of accepting the responsibility for our own leadership. To get the mission accomplished, the goal achieved, and the work done, you need to use all the resources available.

First, establish a vision and guidance for your organization. <u>Share</u> that vision with your followers and yes, even get their input on where the organization should go.

Inspire them to strive to reach the vision. Your inspiration will generally take the form of excitement and enthusiasm for where you are going and what you are doing. If you don't believe in it, why should anyone else?

Give people the tools and resources they need to accomplish the tasks you want them to do. Include information as a resource. People want to know what is going on and how they fit into the overall plan. Along the way, get everyone's input into how you are progressing. Ask people frequently what they need and what they think. You need to be able to see the situation from perspectives other than your own and asking is the only way to gain those other perspectives.

Finally, make sure people are happy in what they do. This can be difficult at times, but is critical to long-term success. Keep in mind that happy people show up – they come to work every day and keep doing so, even when they probably should not. If you have severe absentee problems, chances are that people are not happy in the organization. High turnover rates also indicate you may have a happiness problem. The final indicator is looking at people's faces and truly knowing them as individuals. Happy people smile and are generally pleasant.

Of course, some people who join your organization do not belong there. This happens in every organization. You need to be concerned with them, too. Help them to be happy – somewhere else. People who don't fit in the organization won't be happy there. Maybe the work just does not suit their personalities; maybe their personalities just don't mesh with others. Whatever the case is, help them see they are unhappy and would be happier elsewhere. Generally, these people will see the error of their ways in joining the organization in the first place, and will voluntarily leave. This saves you the unpleasant task of forcing them to leave and ensures they will leave the organization feeling they have been treated fairly.

Chapter Two
The Wheel

Consider your organization a wheel. That is, after all, what this book is all about – viewing your organization as a wheel that rapidly but smoothly rolls along. Most organizations today move very quickly or perish. Therefore, keeping it moving is not necessarily the challenge – business alone usually will take care of that. The key is *steering* or *guiding* that wheel to the proper destination in a way that misses the most potholes, bumps, and other hazards. Please note that I did not say *drive* the wheel. Certainly, leaders often must provide the power to keep the organization going, but great organizations do not rely solely on that power. They rely on other people – the *right* people – business climate, customer demand, and other factors. (Read Good to Great by Jim Collins for more guidance on getting the right people onboard.)

Given that you have the right people to begin with, you'd like to arrive at your destination with all of them still on board and having enjoyed a comfortable ride. You also want to keep the organization moving in the right direction along the way. Consider this: I can drive from Louisville, Kentucky to Cincinnati, Ohio by going north on Interstate 71. It's a relatively short and pleasant drive. We can also get from Louisville to Cincinnati by heading south on I-65 to

Nashville, turning east on I-24 to Knoxville, then north on I-75 through Lexington to Cincinnati. That is obviously a much longer drive, beginning at the same starting point and arriving at the same destination. You could argue that this is an extremely wasteful drive (unless there was a reason in going to these other cities) and I would agree wholeheartedly. So doesn't it make more sense to go straight up I-71 from Louisville to Cincinnati? Without someone planning and steering, however, the vehicle may take the more circuitous route – if it gets to Cincinnati at all! An even better example of this analogy would be to plan the route through smaller towns, staying off Interstate highways altogether. While it might be a much more scenic drive, it would no doubt take much more time and resources to travel the distance.

What does all this have to do with the wheel model of leadership? Just that the wheel is arguably man's greatest invention ever, but as marvelous as it is, all it can do is roll. Without *steering,* it will quickly get off track and end up in the wrong place. Try this: place a simple piece of paper on the floor a few feet away. Now get a single small wheel – from a child's toy, a model, anything – and roll it toward the paper. Repeat this exercise as many times as your sanity and patience will allow. How many times can you make the wheel land on the paper? Probably not many. But you can *steer* that wheel onto the paper every time. Even if you just add an axle and another wheel, you can probably roll this assembly onto the target paper with significantly greater frequency and accuracy. That axle provides enough stability that the wheel(s) roll straight and true, even when you let go.

In this model, the leader is the *axle*, ensuring the wheel stays on track, heading in the proper direction. Axles can also provide driving power, but we are discussing the steering aspect of the axle here. For now, please accept the fact that if leaders alone are providing all the driving power, the wheel will stop moving when the leader is absent. No one can be there all the time. If you are trying to do that, you will burn yourself out.

Figure 1 shows the graphic representation of the model. Note that the people who have contact with *the road* – sales people, customer service representatives, and other production workers – make up the outer surface of the wheel. You can certainly substitute other functions besides what I have shown – you know your organization. These folks make your organization function. They also take the hardest hit when you strike a pothole or hazard. Without them, your wheel is just flat and you are rolling nowhere. You wouldn't drive on tires until all the tread is gone. Don't wear these folks out, either.

Figure 1 – The Wheel

Note also that the leader is in the center of the wheel, serving as the axle. In this position, you can not only steer the direction of the wheel, but also see every part of the organization much better than from any other vantage point.

It is the only point within the circular wheel from which the leader can get to any other point in the least amount of time.

Serving as spokes to connect the leader to the outer rim (production) of the wheel are several parts of the organization. These pieces (or similar pieces) must be in place, as well, to ensure the leader stays connected to what is going on and how the wheel is riding the road. With enough power, even flat, disfigured, or totally shredded wheels can be pushed. Remember, this model is not about power, but about steering with finesse!

Also, consider another wheel – the *steering wheel*. Throughout most of this book, we will discuss the wheel from the aspect of a car's tires, but thinking about the steering wheel helps, as well. Rarely do we yank our cars' steering wheels violently left or right. Rather, we tend to turn them gently, thus smoothly changing directions. Most of us, at some point in time, have experienced one of our front wheels off the edge of a road and had to bring the car back onto the roadway. Some of us did that too abruptly, resulting in dangerous over-steer and over-correction. Fortunately, most of the time we all have the presence of mind and enough experience to get the car back onto the road with no damage or danger, but it is usually a somewhat exciting adventure!

Organizations react the same way – over-steering can cause major disruptions in their direction of travel. Therefore, steering or guiding the organization is generally much smoother and more effective than drastic maneuvers. Such maneuvers are, unfortunately, necessary from time to time but should be the exception, rather than the rule.

Now let's look at the parts of the wheel.

Policies

Policies are fairly broad sets of rules that govern how the organization operates. They are usually prescriptive in nature – such as a retail chain's policy on accepting returned merchandise – but allow for some individual discretion in enforcing them. For example, a local store manager may be able to accept returned merchandise if he or she deems it is the best interest of the store to do so, regardless of the company's over all policy. It may be better to accept the return to ensure the customer's continued business than to enforce a no-return policy and have the customer to shop somewhere else.

Having equitable, fair, and clearly understood policies in place helps the leader steer that outer rim. If properly developed and communicated, they provide a clear understanding of the leader's intent and guidance when the leader is absent. Policies should clarify situations as needed, but cannot possibly cover every eventuality. Trying to ensure they do will only infuse the organization with entirely too many written policies, making them bureaucratic and of no use. Too many organizations have policy manuals that make great doorstops, but nothing else of much value.

Clarity is the key to creating good policies, along with communicating their intent. If the people in your organization understand the intent of your policies, they are more likely to follow them. Give them input into creating the policies and they will ensure the policies make sense and cover only what is needed. Policies help guide the organization and provide sets of rules – paradigms – for others to use in making decisions and reacting to situations when circumstances are unclear. Remember that the people at the periphery of the organization often have a better concept of how things should go than those deeper in the wheel, so get their input into how to take care of customers and situations.

Procedures

As opposed to policies, procedures outline specific steps to take in conducting a transaction, filing information, producing a product, or performing a particular task within the organization. Clear procedures ensure work is done to standard and the consistent quality of your product or service. Well-developed procedures separate and distinguish your company from the competition. They also provide a framework – a road map of sorts – for your workers to follow in producing your product or performing your service.

Procedures, like policies, are prescriptive in nature but usually less adaptive and more restrictive than policies. They describe how you want things done, usually developed and proven effective over time. Standard work ensures consistency, as stated earlier, and lets people know what to do on a day-to-day and hour-to-hour basis. They are, in short, your organization's frame, holding everything together.

The biggest dangers in procedures are having too many, having them too restrictive, or not allowing change. "We've always done it that way" is not a reason to continue performing procedures in the same manner. Do tasks really need to be done a certain way? Sometimes, workers can perform tasks *their* way, instead of yours. For example, if they are making cakes, does it really matter if the sugar goes in before the eggs? If not, don't have a procedure telling them to do it that way. An extreme example of an unnecessary procedure is one telling people how to sweep the floor. Generally, most people do understand how to perform this task. So you probably do not need a formal procedure telling them how. Tell them to do it if necessary. Tell them when, if it is critical to the business, but don't tell them how unless the situation demands it. Doing things your way is not always the best solution. Let people use their own judgment in deciding how to perform tasks. In fact, *train* them to provide input on procedures. Accept the Japanese concept of *kaizen* in your business, which means giving up a little and admitting you don't have all the answers. Tapping into the brainpower and intellectual capacity of your workforce provides you with resources you would otherwise be discarding. Technological advances, changes in customer demands and expectations, and better ideas happen every day. Allowing worker involvement in establishing, maintaining, and modifying procedures is critical to keeping your organization rolling forward and not stagnating. The people who do the work have a unique perspective that you should not dismiss. They will generally find a faster, less expensive way to do things if you allow it. Scrutinize their ideas, of course, but listen to them and encourage them to find better ways to work.

Example

My favorite example of an organization that wasted all of its intellectual capital came as I was working with a company that manufactures small electrical switches, used to ensure your refrigerator light comes on when you open the door and similar applications. The manufacturing process involves winding very small wires on very small fixtures, and is best done by hand. Specifically, the company hired primarily women to perform this task because experience showed that women, because of their smaller hands and manual dexterity, performed better than men did. (Several of them tried to teach me how to do this task and though I am small for a man, I could not do it.)

I was working with the company to help their first-line leaders learn how to train workers more effectively. During the course of the training, I required each student to conduct a short needs analysis, develop a lesson plan and accompanying materials, and conduct a 5 – 15 minute session, usually with me as the student. (They had the

---

option to choose their students, who had to be non-performers on the task. Consequently, most of them chose me. It was great fun.) To aid in the lesson plan development phase, I told them they could use standardized work instructions, which were available for nearly all tasks, rather than having to create separate lesson plan documents.

Their response was that using the work instructions would not work, because that was not how they performed the tasks. I was dumbfounded! When I asked why not, they told me they had found ways of performing most of the tasks that were faster and, in many cases, cheaper and more effective. Excellent! That's how it should work – workers using their experience, intelligence, and problem-solving skills to find better ways to perform. I suggested they modify the work instructions to reflect the improvements. "Oh, we can't do that," they responded, "Management won't let us."

Unfortunately, this situation is far too common in organizations. As far as I know, the company is still there, still manufacturing switches, and still summarily dismissing their workers as stupid, thus ignoring a wonderfully worthwhile and valuable resource.

Your procedures have to address enough to get the work done, obviously. They must provide sufficient detail to ensure quality. They do differentiate your organization from similar ones. (If you are operating a Burger King, you do not necessarily want to make McDonald's hamburgers.) Often, however, they inhibit growth, innovation and initiative. So take a good, long look at your procedures to ensure they serve to hold your organization together without simultaneously holding it back.

Subordinate Leaders

Leadership starts at the top, but runs throughout the organization. Regardless of how many official leaders you have at any and all levels of the organization, leadership occurs. You need to accept that fact right away. Of course, most organizations have mid-managers, first-line supervisors, and maybe senior managers or executives. Smaller organizations may not have as many levels or as many people at each of the levels, but there are usually people other than you serving the organization in a leadership capacity. Even if there are not, leadership is taking place, either officially or unofficially, at all levels within the organization. It is inevitable if there are people there.

Let me take a moment at this point to reiterate that we are discussing *effective leadership* here. As I pointed out in the first chapter, the definition of effective leadership varies greatly between people – even between the "experts." Regardless of whether or not you accept the definition I offered, *effective leadership, management,* and *supervision* are distinctly different. Were it within my power and capabilities, I would immediately wave my magic wand and make all organizational position titles accurately reflect the positions.

Some of your mid-managers are, in fact, managers. They *manage*, ensuring proper stewardship of the organization's resources – money, raw materials, products or services in production, finished products, time, whatever. With the cost of everything today, management is extremely important to the financial well-being of the organization. We live in an expensive age that promises to get even more expensive. I am not suggesting that you lessen the management in your organization. It is critical.

In many cases, however, organizations assume that managing and leading are the same functions, requiring the same skills. They are not and they do not. Trying to manage people is like trying to herd cats – it doesn't work and generally results in frustrating all parties involved. People want you to lead them, not manage them. Let me give you an example:

Within your organization, you know that the workload requirement for Section A, which has six people, will be down to about a four-person level over the next month. Concurrently, Section B, also with six people, is facing an eight-person workload for the same period. This simple human resource management challenge has a simple solution: move two people from Section A to Section B for the time involved. When the workload stabilizes, everyone reverts to his or her usual assignment. This is a management decision.

Now, actually communicating this decision to the people affected is a *leadership* action. You can abruptly tell them to report to the other section and ignore how they feel about the change or you can recognize that you are asking them to do something above and beyond their usual duties, acknowledge their efforts, and enhance their motivation in the process. *How* you direct people in the accomplishment of this little HR management challenge, how you communicate your management decision to the people involved is a *leadership* challenge.

Finally, *supervision* involves watching and monitoring others. While I do not pretend that monitoring is not necessary, *supervision* is required and better performed with two-year-olds. They need constant watching. Adult workers neither need nor desire supervision. Remember from Chapter 1 that effective leaders help workers remain happy. If you have a worker who requires supervision, you need to help him be happy – somewhere else. He does not belong in your organization if you must spend your time supervising. You need people who can work independently with the proper leadership, not those requiring constant supervision.

Having digressed into a discussion of the differences between terms often considered synonymous, let's now address how subordinate leaders serve to keep your wheel rolling. Collectively, they are one of the spokes of your wheel, which will roll a bit like an egg without them, or even with them if used inappropriately or ineffectively. Simply, you cannot be everywhere all the time. Most organizations are far too complex for one person – you – to effectively make all the decisions and personally lead everyone. Your subordinate leaders provide a conduit through which you communicate the policies and procedures we discussed earlier. They also serve to enforce those policies and procedures when required, keep you informed of what is going on in all parts of the organization, and generally become extensions of your decision-making authority within their portions of the organization. Use them, trust them, groom them. Don't forget that these people need training, too. You should develop them for positions of greater responsibility nearly continuously. Allow them to make decisions commensurate with their experience and capabilities, and challenge them to perform. Remember that they will make mistakes, too. Allow it and gently help them learn from those mistakes.

Since leadership starts at the top, your subordinate leaders will tend to lead the way you lead. If you want them to be open, innovative, motivating leaders, you should lead that way. If you are an uncaring, autocratic, non-communicative tyrant, they will tend to lead that way, as well. If, however, you want subordinate leaders who are open, innovative, and focused on effectively performing the three functions we identified in Chapter 1, model the behaviors you expect in them. Setting the example is an incredibly powerful factor in leadership, will earn you respect and trust, and if done properly, empowers your subordinate leaders, thus making your job easier.

You would not ask a carpenter to build a house without a hammer. Don't ask your subordinate leaders to build the organizational wheel without the proper tools, either. Give them the training and tools they need to be effective, including commensurate authority. Nothing builds confidence and trust in mid-level and first-line leaders like allowing them appropriate authority. Granting it gains and enhances their respect and trust in you, as well as helping them gain the trust and respect of subordinate workers.

Send them to training seminars, hire a leadership training consultant, create a leadership development reading list, do all of these if necessary, but give them the skills and tools they need to be successful. When possible, promote from within. Doing so capitalizes on development investments you have already spent on people and provides motivation for the entire organization. Most people like promotions and will perform better if they feel there is something to gain from their hard work. On the other hand, if they feel trapped in a dead-end position, what is the point of their trying to improve themselves or the organization?

Of course, there is another potential cost to developing leaders. Many senior leaders I have worked with fear that giving subordinates more skills and capabilities makes them more likely to leave the organization. In these cases, the resources spent on development become costs, rater than investments. However, experience has shown that quite often people – particularly younger leaders – will stay where they feel they are likely to get more development opportunities. Their loyalties often lie in their own abilities and skills, rather than in the organization. They stay where they feel they can gain more skills. Without going too deeply into organizational history, this is probably due to having seen their parents swept aside by companies during the downsizing of the 1980s and 1990s. (This is completely my unscientific theory, based on reading numerous articles and speaking with hundreds of younger workers, but it is my story and I am sticking to it!) The bottom line is to develop your subordinates to practice your desired leadership practices – don't expect them to just lead that way intuitively. Too many times, we promote excellent workers into leadership roles without giving them the necessary skills or tools to be successful.

Your subordinate leaders function as a critical link between you and the rest of the organization. You simply cannot be everywhere all the time. If developed and trained to perform their leadership responsibilities in a manner supporting your leadership climate and the organizational personality as a whole, these people become your presence throughout the organization. Add in their innate intelligence and innovation, and they are a powerfully positive force.

Communication

I discuss communication as the last spoke in the wheel because it is the most important, the most overlooked, and the most common cause of problems. Quite often, leaders just assume that everyone throughout the organization has all the information required to do perform appropriately. Even more frequently, that assumption is incorrect. Having consulted with hundreds of organizations, I can say (again, unscientifically) that communication is the cause of problems in effective operations the great majority of the time. Usually, the only definitive thing we can say about organizational communications is that they can improve. The larger and more complex the organization, the more difficult effective communication becomes. Adding people to the situation seems to have an exponential effect on communications issues.

So how do you use communication to steer the wheel? If communication is such a problem, how can it be one of the spokes that hold the wheel together? Well, organizations that communicate well have a basic advantage over their competitors. Effective communication ensures everyone in the organization has the information she or he needs. This doesn't mean everyone needs to know everything, though the more people know about the system in which they are working, the better they understand the entire operation, and the better they can perform within that system. People who know how they and what they do fit into the big picture feel more connected, more part of the whole operation, and more vital to the organization's ultimate success.

You strengthen and improve communication in the organization in several ways. First, *be accessible*. You cannot communicate directly with people from your office. You have to get out occasionally and walk on the street, where the rubber meets the road. (Please forgive the cliché. It just fits so well here!) Open door policies have different effects than being out among people in their own environments. Not only are they more willing to discuss real issues with you because of simple familiarity, but also you gain a better understanding of how the organization is functioning. Being on the outer rim occasionally also keeps you connected to your customers, and without them, there is no point in the organization in the first place. It also tells people – workers and customers – that you know they are there, understand their worlds, and care about them as people.

Keep in mind that these visits to the rim of the wheel should be non-threatening, relatively frequent, and unannounced. Just showing up communicates a great deal. Announcing that you are going to be in a certain area at a certain time says, "I'm coming and want you to prepare for this auspicious occasion." Appearing unannounced, however, says, "I know you are here and just wanted to say hello and see how you are doing. I care about you." Remember this word of caution, though: if you consistently just correct people or catch them dong something wrong, your efforts to be present in their worlds may have the reverse effect. If people think you are just checking up on them, they will be constantly defensive and much less inclined to be innovative or to take risks to try to improve. How frequently you make these visits depends entirely on your schedule and the tempo of the operation, but they should be frequent within those parameters. Being non-threatening means asking people what they need from you and ensuring their welfare, not inspecting them as though they need close supervision.

Another tactic to enhance communication is to *over-communicate*. Tell your immediate subordinates more information than they need. Remember, the more they know about the operation, the better they will be able to perform. Ensure they, too, over-communicate with their subordinates. The old adage that "knowledge is power" is very true, especially in this information age. Knowledge is much more powerful, however, when shared. If only you have certain information, that knowledge can be applied and leveraged in any given situation only if you are there. If it is spread widely throughout the organization, almost any member at any level of the organization can apply knowledge in almost any situation. If in doubt as to whether people need a given piece of information, give it to them. Then get their feedback to give you an idea of when you are reaching information overload. In other words, let them help filter out what they do not need and help find the appropriate balance.

Of course, you communicate in other ways, too. Newsletters, bulletin boards, memos, meetings, and many other media disseminate pertinent bits of information. All are important and useful. The key is to use them effectively and encourage communication throughout the organization. Don't over look lateral communication. Encourage managers and leaders at every level to coordinate matters between themselves without having to bring them higher. This ensures they understand and get to know each other and relieves you of unnecessary time-consuming activities. They can and should inform you of problems they have resolved or averted, but certainly can do so without your direct involvement.

Remember that when it comes to communication, your goal is to ensure understanding. Constantly check for understanding, but never ask the question "do you understand?" The answer is nearly always a resounding "yes," for one of several reasons. First, the other person or persons may think they do understand, and thus answer accordingly. Maybe they were not listening, but not want you to realize it. There are many reasons people answer "yes" to the question "do you understand," all of which are valid. Your goal is to ensure they do understand. Do that by asking the right questions. Rather than ask "do you understand," try saying "I sometimes don't express myself well enough, so please tell me what you think I want from you. I don't mean to insult your intelligence, but we need to ensure we understand the same thing," or words to that effect. This will feel rather strange the first few times you do it – for both you and the other person. With practice, however, all concerned will become used to it and appreciate the shared understanding that results.

Example

While I was still in the Army, my boss collared me one day with the instructions that the general needed something, and I was going to be the one to do it. "Come with me," he said, "so we can hear what he wants." Off we went down the hall to the "old man's" office to get our guidance.

Entering the office, my boss told the general I was here to get guidance on what it was he needed us to do. The general agreed to my being the one to accomplish the task in question – coordinating input from several key staff officers and writing an urgent document – then launched into his specific guidance on what the document should say.

You need to know here that those of us who worked in the headquarters knew this particular general to have a relatively short, but very deep attention span. Understandably, he did not appreciate having to repeat himself, but also was very conscious of communication issues and respected the fact that other people worked hard,

---

too. After several minutes of my taking notes as he explained his guidance, he dismissed the two of us to go forth and do great things with the project.

Before leaving, however, I stopped.

"Excuse me, sir, but could I just make sure I know what it is you want me to do?" I asked. I looked at his somewhat incredulous face and thought I might have made a mistake, though I had worked with him for some time and felt I was within reason. After several very long moments, he spoke.

"Jeff, why did you ask me that?" he asked.

"It's really pretty simple, sir," I responded. "There are two reasons, actually. First, I am busy and don't want to have to do it twice. Also, I have seen people bring you projects that are not what you have asked for. It's not pretty and I don't want to go there!"

He took great delight in this and laughed, joined by the colonel and me.

"Jeff, why can't I get all these colonels who work for me to be that clear?" the general asked. "It would sure make things smoother."

"I don't know, sir. I'm afraid they're not my problem," I said, which elicited another laugh.

> "No, you're right – they're my problem. Now, what is it you need to know?"
>
> I went through my notes to ensure I had captured his main points, returned to my office, and handled the project. Had I not ensured understanding, however, that project most likely would have been much harder work. In this case, I was the follower, not the leader, ensuring understanding. But it worked.

Understand that perception is reality when it comes to communication. The leader of an organization once told me "we don't have a communication problem in my organization, but some of our people think we do." In the ensuing conversation, it took me a couple hours to convince him that he, indeed, did have a communication problem. He was convinced that no problem existed because he understood what he wanted. A lack of understanding within the organization obviously meant that those who did not understand were stupid, did not want to understand, were not paying attention, or some combination thereof. Communication requires a sender and a receiver, both of whom share in the responsibility of ensuring understanding, but the sender has the primary responsibility. After all, he is the one initiating the message.

Finally, understand that you never cease to communicate. Sitting in your office and leaving everyone alone sends a message, however the receivers perceive it. Absence, over-supervision, and friendliness all communicate. Your challenge is to communicate the message you intend.

Summary

Viewing your organization as a rolling wheel helps you understand the speed at which it moves and the stresses occurring at the outer rim. Your performing as the axle of that wheel keeps it moving in the desired direction and at the proper speed. Policies, procedures, subordinate leaders, and communication hold the wheel together and transmit the power from the axle to the outer edge. Ensuring these spokes are properly tuned and maintained makes your job as a leader easier and the entire organization more effective.

The remaining chapters of this book address specific situations within the organization and how to adapt this model to them. No model works 100% of the time for all organizations, so feel free to choose which pieces you will use. I do not mean it as a panacea for all problems.

Chapter Three
The Wheel and the Absent Leader

You accept that as the axle in your organizational wheel, you have to provide a vision that inspires people, ensure they have the tools necessary to succeed, and yes, even keep them happy. For the moment, at least, you also accept that policies, procedures, communication, and subordinate leaders are the "spokes" that help you hold the whole organization together. You even accept that the workers are out where the rubber meets the road and the only ones separating you from the hot, hard, brutal road. Without them, you can go nowhere; you know that.

So what happens when you are not there? You cannot be everywhere all the time – we have established that. You do have to leave the immediate work area occasionally making sales and sealing deals, meeting with customers, suppliers or the boss, or even just to see your kid play soccer. (Yes, there is life beyond work. If this is news to you, you have other problems. I'll write another book for that later.) Who or what guides the wheel when you are elsewhere? Sure, those subordinate leaders we discussed are there and quite capable, but some things require central guidance – an axle's job. How can you guide the wheel when you are somewhere else?

You may even be within the organization, but attending to an issue in one section or department when a different problem arises in another department. Do you abandon the original issue to resolve the new problem, hoping the original problem will wait? Do you resolve the original problem first and pray the new issue gets no worse in the interim? Being out in the organization is critical to maintaining visibility and resolving the inevitable challenges that occur every day. However, off-center axles transform wheels into cams that tend not to roll very smoothly.

You can create cams without trying or even being aware of it, so be careful. Say, for instance, that you came from the sales department. That is where you spent much of your developmental career before becoming the axle. (Keep in mind there are smaller axles and smaller wheels arranged throughout your big wheel.) Having come from sales, you feel a fond affinity for them and spend an inordinate amount of time there, partially because you understand that part of the business better than others and partially because you understand the people there. Being in the sales department so much means you may be neglecting other departments, thus putting the axle off-center in the wheel. What ensures the wheel does not turn into a cam and careen into oblivion?

Strong *shared values* are the answer. When the same values are important to everyone in the organization – throughout the wheel – it will stay on course regardless of whether the leader is physically there. This is not to say that you, as the leader, just go in, establish values, leave, and live happily ever after while the wheel rolls itself smoothly down the road. Unfortunately, bumps and potholes in the road, unexpected detours, changes in speed limits, and other variables do require your being there frequently. Values do not replace leadership. When you cannot be there, however, values provide the framework enabling others to make decisions consistent with the organization's direction and vision. Values do not replace the leader; they define the leader.

Of course, this requires that everyone knows and accepts the values. Remember that I referred to them as *shared* values. Personal values are great – they make us who we are and add to the glorious diversity of life on our planet. Organizations, however, need a set of values running through their center – their axles – to help everyone within those organizations head in the same direction. Multiple sets of personal values all guiding individual actions simultaneously have a tendency to foster chaos and conflict, not productivity.

While having valuable members of the organization with clearly defined personal values is wonderful, only *shared* values can provide the absent leader with a directional safety net.

Clearly defining shared values for the organization as the leader is not simple. It requires time and effort, open communication with all segments of the organization, and the willingness to accept input from other members. Trying to impose values does not make them shared values. Printing them on lovely stationery, framing them, and hanging them throughout the facility likewise do not guarantee they are shared values. The organization must instill and internalize values throughout for them to work. People must truly believe stated values for them to be effective.

As people, we behave according to our values. Merely saying we value something is unconvincing if that statement conflicts with our behaviors. This is why people believe what they see, not what they hear. We all do it, and rightfully so. Think of a time you heard someone say something and thought "yeah, right. That will be the day!" You found the statement hard to believe because the speaker's actions and words did not match. The speaker was stating what he or she wanted you to hear and maybe even meant it sincerely. You believed the behavior, not the words. Pardon my resorting to clichés, but actions really do speak louder than words. (You know, most clichés actually do contain an element of truth! That is, after all, how they become clichés in the first place.)

Truly shared values require input from everyone in the organization, or at least every segment. When everyone buys into one set of values, amazing things happen. Interpersonal conflict decreases. Productivity increases. Everyone cares about what he or she is doing to further the organization's performance of its mission. People are happier when they are working with others who share the same values and happy people are more productive. Shared values help create a sharp focus for the organization, providing a barometer for what is best for the entire organization and empowering people at all levels to make appropriate decisions clearly.

To create, instill, and internalize shared values within your organization, take the time to talk to people. Gather the "movers and shakers" from all parts of the organization in the same room and spend the time necessary to draft some shared values. Make them simple enough to remember, but in-depth enough to mean something significant to everyone. Then give these movers and shakers time to field the ideas to the rest of the organization before you reconvene and refine the list. Be open to accepting new values that your group may not have considered the first time, but about which someone else felt strongly. Again, spend the time to discuss all aspects of the process and create a set of values truly shared by everyone. Once the set of values is set and clarified, share them with everyone. Make it a celebration! Then live them.

This is the hard part – keeping focused on these values as the pressures of competition and daily life come to bear. Well-developed values will stand the pressure and scrutiny. However, they require reinforcement. If they are truly internalized, real live, breathing values, this is not hard at all. The values guide your actions and those of other leaders, everyone sees the resultant behavior, and you set the example for the rest of the organization.

Once the values are deeply instilled and embedded within the organization, the leader's absence does not create a gaping hole in guidance and decision-making. The values serve as the axle, keeping the wheel on a steady track, or at least headed in the right direction. Not having to rely solely on the leader for specific guidance at every turn, the people within the wheel correct small imbalances and deviations themselves, guided by the knowledge that they know what is important to the organization through widespread acceptance of shared values.

A good set of shared values has the added benefit of acting as the lubricant or grease between leaders and others within the organization. When the same values are important to everyone in the organization, the friction causing conflict decreases. Obviously, there will always be disagreements and interpersonal conflict in organizations – it is the nature of humans to disagree – but strong shared values provide a focus, a filter of sorts, to clarify and simplify many common conflicts.

Example

While in one position in the Army, I used what I called a "filter" to test the values against what we were doing. This was in the early '90s, when the Army was nearing the end of a period of downsizing, and my major command (Training and Doctrine Command – TRADOC) had repeatedly lost positions. The organizational structure was stretched so thin that we could barely accomplish existing missions and were having great difficulty accepting new ones.

The job I had primarily involved managing the training of approximately 20,000 soldiers a year. My organization, consisting mostly of civilian professional-level employees, was as thin as every other similar organization. As the chief of a staff section, my primary responsibilities were managing workflow and establishing priorities. (And often what I referred to as "keeping the wolves away" so the extremely competent personnel in the section could do their work without having to worry about anything else.) In establishing the priorities, my filter was usually the question "how does this train soldiers?" If we could not answer the question adequately, we took steps to stop doing whatever task was in question.

Occasionally my boss illustrated to me how a task did contribute to training soldiers and was, therefore, worthy of our time. More often, however, he backed me up and supported my decision to stop performing tasks for which we could not make that connection.

The shared value of focusing on our primary mission of training soldiers kept all of us on track with doing what was right and made sense, and allowed us to filter out superfluous bureaucratic "busy work." Without that focus –

that shared value – we would have spun our wheels a lot and accomplished much less meaningful work.

I cannot overemphasize the importance of well-developed and well-communicated shared values. They literally transform organizations from chaos into well-oiled, finely tuned mechanisms. They define the organization and set it apart from competitors. Whether a business or a non-profit, a municipal government or an educational institution, every organization needs shared values. And everyone in those organizations needs to understand and buy into those values. When that happens, leadership blossoms and flourishes.

Another Army Example

As a young officer just beginning my career and my adventure in leadership, I was nervous preparing for my first big inspection – three days after reporting into my first unit. Determined to make an impression and ensure my superiors I was a competent leader, I walked into the platoon area ready to take charge. Very quickly, I realized that preparations were well under way for the inspection. Soldiers I didn't even know yet were scurrying everywhere, obviously intent upon whatever task the noncommissioned officers (NCOs) had given them. Within my first real day on the job, I admitted to my platoon sergeant, the senior NCO in the platoon, that I did not know what was going on. What happened then was my first real lesson in leadership, which I will never forget.

He told me, "Sir, you're not supposed to know what's going on. That's why you're here. Trust me; I'll show you what's going on and what your job is."

What? "I'm in charge. I'm the one who is supposed to be running things," I thought to myself. Then I made one of the smartest leadership decisions of my career – I took him up on the offer. Maybe I was making a mistake, but I decided to trust this man.

Three days later, the Commanding General (CG) arrived at our platoon for the inspection. When he entered the platoon area I saluted smartly and said, "Sir, welcome to First Platoon. I'm Lieutenant Corkran and I have been here three days, so I don't really even know what is going on. If you don't mind, I'd like to allow Sergeant Tatman to lead you through our area on the inspection." Then I waited for the general to tell me I was the Platoon Leader and should be able to handle such a task. But he didn't. Instead, he looked at me, winked, and said "I don't mind at all, Lieutenant. Smart man."

Then the CG went to talk to the soldiers. Sure, he inspected them and their carefully prepared equipment, but what he really wanted was to hear what they had to say because he *valued* that information. He knew through extensive experience that our unit depended on the soldiers being happy, being cared for, and being well trained. He also knew that leaders in the organization might tell him what they thought he wanted to hear. He <u>knew</u> the soldiers would not do that. They would tell him the truth. He was trying to instill and share a value of caring for, challenging, and training soldiers properly.

60

Chapter Four
The Wheel Compared to other Leadership
Models

Why do we need another leadership model? With plenty of them out there, organizations have been functioning perfectly well for many years. What does *The Wheel* offer that is different or innovative? Just another perspective. Not earth shattering, this model does fit the early 21st Century in a way that makes sense. When organizations took years to change, the old models worked fine. When life moved at a slower pace, leaders were able to look around, notice the change, and adapt accordingly. Change occurs more rapidly now and leaders need to be able to adapt, change, and *steer* their organizations rapidly to adjust to that change and keep pace with the competition.

The most traditional model for leadership that I know of is the pyramid shown in figure 2. With the leader at the top, above managers, supervisors, and workers, this model is quite familiar. Of course, most organizations have more layers than depicted here, but you get the point. Certainly, leaders are at the top of their organizations in most cases. I'm sure there is a great view from up there, but how much of what is going on in the organization can the leader see? The levels of bureaucracy (did I actually write that?) have a way of insulating and isolating the leader from the rest of the people involved in making the organization function properly.

Oh, I know, "my door is always open." Sure it is, if someone wants to climb all the way up there. Let's face it, pyramids and triangles, though geometrically extremely stable, don't turn or roll very well.

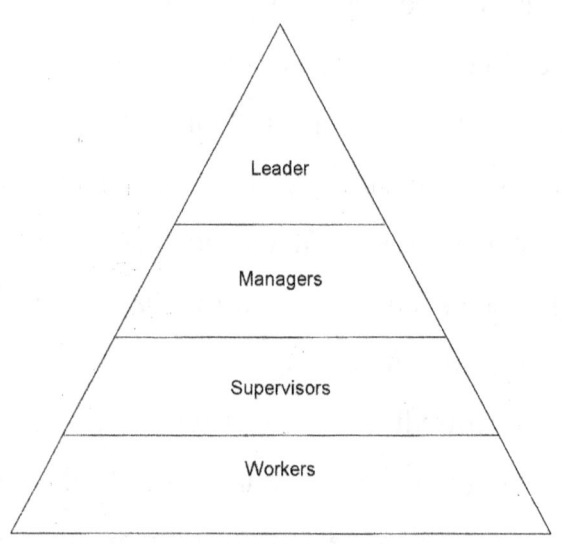

Figure 2 – The Pyramid

The pyramid has served us well over the years. Many fine businesses, governments, churches, non-profit organizations, and other entities were built on this model of leadership. The problem is that it just doesn't fit anymore. Society rarely works that way in this century. All of us want a say in what goes on. So let's allow the trusty old pyramid to retire, and while you may remember it well, try not to let it work its way into your thinking on leadership.

Servant leadership – that's the answer! That notion has been around a while. Robert Greenleaf coined the phrase in 1970, but the idea has been around much, much longer. Although commonly attributed to Jesus, servant leadership also appears in several Eastern writings older than the New Testament. Surely, a concept and model that has survived that long must be worth keeping. Yes. And no. Servant leadership absolutely has its place in society. Many leaders and organizations practice this style of leadership very well and very effectively.

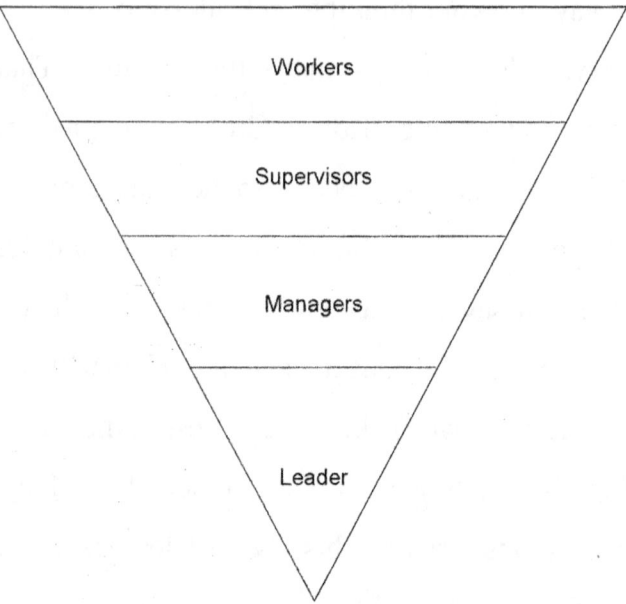

Figure 3 – Servant Leadership

The major problem with servant leadership in most organizations is that the leader, at the bottom of the inverted pyramid, is shouldering the entire load. Many strong leaders can do this effectively, but for how long? Such practice sounds to me like a good way to wear out an otherwise wonderful leader. Certainly, this style of leadership works in many situations and members of organizations whose leaders who lead in this manner generally feel appreciated and happy. This model does emphasize the dignity of the individual, ethical uses of authority, collaboration, and understanding people as people.

However, this model does not address the communications issues that a hierarchical pyramid presents any more effectively than the traditional model does. Still displaced from the day-to-day action the leader's communications still must pass through several levels between the leader and employees, workers, volunteers, or whoever is at the "worker" level in your organization.

Understand that I am not criticizing the *philosophy* of servant leadership. In the first chapter, I stated that effective leaders provide the tools and resources, including information that people need to be successful. They also devote energy and attention to keeping people happy and satisfied within the organization. These concepts clearly fit within a servant leadership mind set. The *model* is the problem. Seeing the organization as pyramid may have worked well in ancient Egypt, but that perspective does not fit life adequately in the 21st Century. Therefore, if thinking of yourself as a servant leader helps you stay focused, please do so. Just think about how well – or how poorly – that pyramid will "move" in operating the organization.

Maybe much more prevalent in today's world, organization charts provide a great way to see the functional relationships of the different parts of the organization. They clearly illustrate how the organizational pieces fit together. However, as a leadership model, these charts still tend to separate the parts of the organization and keep the leader isolated. Communication tends to follow the lines of the chart, which is perfectly acceptable in many cases but can become a problem when the leader needs to communicate directly with individuals within those sections.

Figure 4 shows an example of an organizational chart. Look at the distance and levels between the leader and a member of the lower subsection under personnel recruiting. That's a long way! Of course, nothing stops the leader from leaving his top block and communicating directly with someone in that section, but the chart *as a model* suggests the communication should follow the lines between levels. Given that these levels also have leaders – the subordinate leaders discussed as a spoke in Chapter One – communication becomes difficult. Leaders certainly need to keep the subordinate leaders informed and involved in what is going on, but they should also not hamper direct communication when it is necessary. Again, as a model for leadership, the chart fails to keep things rolling.

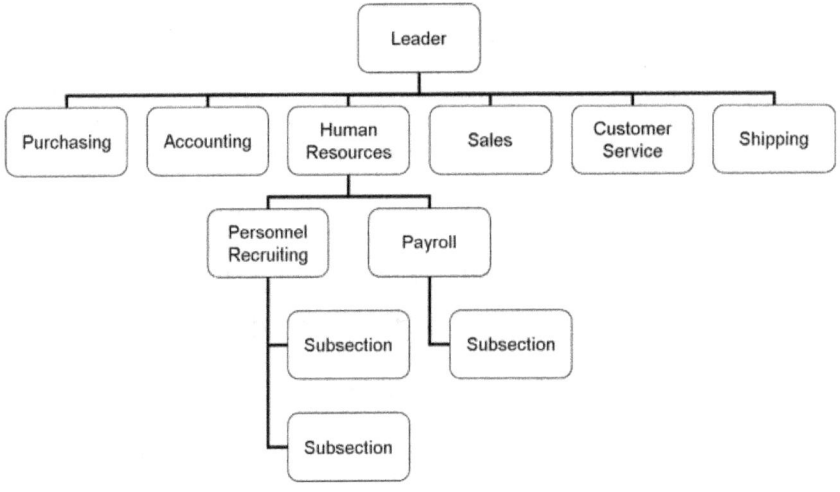

Figure 4 – Organizational Chart

Let's address leadership *philosophy* again. Keep in mind that your personal philosophy of leadership fits into any of these models. Your personality and leadership behaviors greatly influence your effectiveness as a leader, regardless of the model you follow. *The Wheel* does not replace good leadership practices, for which there are literally thousand of other books to help you grow and develop. The model does define the leadership process within the organization in a slightly different perspective to try to help you cope with being a leader in today's fast-paced world.

Unfortunately, organizations really do need, well, organization. Organizational charts are a well-accepted way to depict the relationships of one section, department, or office to another. Please don't misunderstand – I am not trying to tell you to throw out all your charts or to allow chaos to reign supreme. I am just trying to point out the flaws of using such charts as a defining leadership model. Charts do have their useful place in any organization. If we can agree to use an organizational chart as shown in figure 5, I can live with that, providing the leader understands that he must move throughout the organization and not stay isolated in the middle!

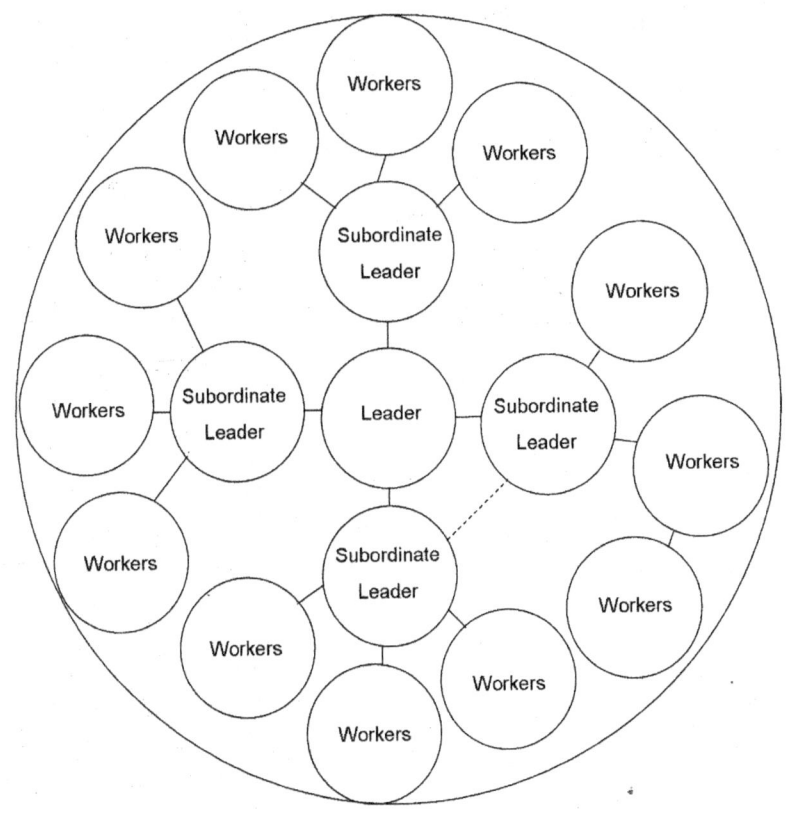

Figure 5 – An Alternate Organization Chart

To finish this chapter, let me address Situational Leadership as defined by Paul Hersey and Ken Blanchard. Effective leadership is <u>never</u> one-size-fits-all. Truly effective leaders recognize that people differ, situations change, and conditions are not always clear, and they adjust their leadership styles and behaviors accordingly. Hersey and Blanchard recognized this and provided an excellent

71

framework to help you adapt to such changes. Again, *The Wheel* does not negate their wonderfully insightful points or suggest alternate behaviors as appropriate. It merely provides a different view on the organizational framework in which situational leaders operate.

Chapter Five
The Wheel and Your Boss

Having read this far, you may have decided to try this wheel idea. You'll spend some time making sure you provide clear guidance, inspire a shared vision, develop shared values, provide people the resources they need to be successful, and find out what will help people be happy. You can do that. Getting out into the organization is a good idea anyway – you have been meaning to do more of that. You are always looking for new ways to be a better leader. Why not try this? Wait, there's a problem. Sure, *you* can be this kind of leader but your boss will never buy off on the idea. Unless he or she changes, how can you? The constant pressure, the boss's focus on everything that goes wrong, his tendency to "keep people in line" will certainly hamper your efforts to change, won't they?

In short, no. Your decision to change your leadership style certainly comes at a cost. Effective leadership is not for the feint of heart – it requires courage and commitment. Regardless of the leadership behaviors your boss chooses to practice, you make your own decisions concerning your own behaviors. Those decisions may or may not be popular or even accepted by your boss, so you also must decide if you are going to allow your boss to steer your organizational leadership wheel or do it yourself. I prefer to make those decisions for myself and brave the potholes and swerves necessary to stay my own course. Decide for yourself, but do so with the understanding that "bucking the system" indeed may result in some resistance from above. Many leaders find it quite threatening to have subordinate leaders practice better leadership skills than they do, and will take actions to ensure the potholes are deep enough to swallow the offending subordinate. As I said, improving your leadership style is not without its dangers.

Of course, having a boss who does practice caring, informed, liberating leadership is of great value. Find those types of leaders in the organization, whether they are your bosses or not, and emulate them. Ask them for guidance and support. Ask them what they did when faced with an unenlightened boss who did not approve of their style of leadership. They will most likely be very willing to share any secrets they may have and will be quite flattered that you have asked. Ask these people to mentor you. Tell them you want to learn more. Part of providing the resources that people need to be successful is helping them develop as leaders and grow in their value to the organization.

Throughout this discussion, remember that there are formal leaders and informal leaders. Don't worry about titles such as manager or chief. Leadership is about influencing others, and many people are excellent at steering the wheel without ever having been given the official keys to the vehicle. Start with gaining the leadership skills rather than with getting the job with the title. Chances are that the job and title will follow if you are committed to practicing the skills. Effective leadership has a way of showing in organizations. Someone will notice your efforts.

Having someone notice is also part of leadership. Make sure you highlight the accomplishments of others. I'm not suggesting you toot your own horn all the time – that usually does not characterize an effective leader. What I am suggesting is that you make sure your team, department, section, or whatever – *"your"* – receives due credit for what they do. Sharing the glory of accomplishments is an integral part of leading effectively. Practice it long enough and someone will notice effective leadership.

Exactly what they will notice is a different story. Remember that leading this way requires courage. Sometimes, you will have to stand up for what you believe is right. That may mean disagreeing with your boss or other people of authority in the organization. Occasionally, you will lose these battles – expect it. Pick your battles wisely and only when they really matter. Some just aren't worth the effort. Be sure to stand up for your subordinates, whether they are right or wrong. What, stand up for someone who is wrong? Yes. Backing them when they make bad decisions ensures these people that you have their best interests at heart. They need to understand when their judgment or decisions are not appropriate or tight, but you need to support them regardless.

Example

In one position early in my career, I inherited a work section with a somewhat bad reputation. In beginning the job, it quickly became clear that the biggest problem was that my predecessor had not supported and encouraged the workers within the section. He spent his time pointing out mistakes and failures rather than building on strength and success. Consequently, he failed to create trust and rapport within the organization. I decided I would turn that around by focusing on accomplishments.

I am not suggesting that I totally disregarded the failures. My focus, however, was on success. In fact, I made a small sign for my desk saying "The buck stops here... but I make change." I wanted them to know that if

---

they screwed up and did something wrong, my boss would never hear about it. (This was relative, of course. I was not in the practice or habit of protecting criminals.) Minor infractions of rules or poor performance, however, were my domain. I would take the hit from the boss – the buck – if someone did something improperly. The offending individual would then privately hear from me how to correct his performance problem and avoid it the next time. That was the change.

It worked. Within a few months, personnel within the section were behaving as a team and our reputation improved. I took a few hits from the boss, but seem to have recovered from them. The members of the team appreciated my willingness to support them and develop their skills, and responded by improving their performance. Of course, I did not accomplish all this alone. Subordinate leaders quickly bought into the idea and supported the team's members, as well. It takes the whole team to make it work. All I did was establish the leadership climate within the section, and it wasn't necessarily easy. My boss was a my-way-or-the-highway type who consistently spent much of the day trying to catch people doing something wrong. He advised me numerous times that I should be doing the same thing to maintain the pressure. I persisted and accomplished most of what I intended to achieve.

Being an effective leader is not easy. It is tough, daunting work, requiring courage, inspiration, and perseverance. Depending on your leader's attitude, it may also require swimming upstream a few times. Hopefully, your boss understands effective leadership and provides you the same guidance and support you are trying to show your subordinates. Unfortunately, that is not always the case. Regardless of the leadership climate in which you work, you ultimately decide how you will lead and what behaviors and attitudes you will adopt. Keeping the good of the organization and the people at the center of your decisions will help you achieve this situation. Remembering and modeling the shared values you have created and agreed to provide the consistency your subordinates want and expect.

Chapter Six

The Wheel and the New Leader –

Starting Right

Your initial behavior upon becoming a leader is critical to your success throughout the remainder of your leadership career. As with many other practices, beginning to lead properly is usually better than re-learning and having to change behaviors later. How you choose to lead in your first leadership role sets the tone for how you will tend to lead in progressively more responsible positions. Consequently, getting the right tone or leadership climate has a great affect on your over all success.

Generally, there are two ways we become leaders: we receive a promotion from within or join a new organization as a leader based on experience gained somewhere else. Either way is difficult. First, let me say that I firmly support internal promotions. Internal promotion policies capitalize on organizational knowledge and communicate to the members of that organization that there is potential for growth and development. People who see that they can gain and progress in an organization are more likely to want to achieve and succeed in that organization, and will thus be more productive. Especially when the organizational culture supports and encourages effective leadership development and growth, internal promotion policies foster "grow-your-own" self-sustainment. By developing and promoting potential leaders, the organization capitalizes on past training and experience, ultimately saving time and money.

Individuals receiving such promotions, however, need to understand there are costs involved in such actions. In even the best organizations, some amount of "we/they" always exists. Becoming "the boss" may mean you are no longer "one of the guys." Suddenly, you are one of "them." It can be quite a startling discovery to find the people with whom you have always shared everything and spoken freely now tend to speak to you differently and not be as forthcoming about their activities. They may react differently when approached about problems or when questioned about their productivity. After all, you are now someone perceived as wanting more from them, without any additional compensation of any kind. It can be quite a lonely experience.

Another side to this internal promotion coin is that "the guys" may expect you to show them more favoritism than the previous supervisor, boss, manager, or leader. After all, you know what they are experiencing and should sympathize with them. Unfortunately, you now have a slightly different perspective on the situation and received the promotion because someone believes you can get the job done effectively. Playing favorites is seldom part of the situation. Your old co-workers cannot understand your apparent change of loyalties and your boss expects results. Balancing these new relationships and expectations can be very tricky.

Coming into a new organization as a leader is equally tricky, but in different ways. In this case, you must learn the way the new organization does business – whatever that business may be – in addition to learning new names, personalities, and requirements. Whatever your previous experience, you are "the new guy" who must prove himself or herself. Others may see you as believing they have done things wrong in the past, which you plan to fix, or they may believe you just know nothing. Either way, you have a tough situation. You simultaneously have to establish rapport with everyone, learn the new organization and its mission, and establish your credibility as a leader.

So which is better for the new leader: promotion from within or beginning a leadership career in a new organization? Whatever circumstances present you with a leadership opportunity are better for you. Personally, I believe promotion from within is usually the preferred route. Despite the challenges discussed earlier, there is simply less to learn. Knowing the organization, its mission, and the existing leadership climate provide the leader with a foundation on which to build. Unfortunately, that same leader must also overcome old habits developed as an employee and learn new relationships with old co-workers and new peers. As I mentioned – the situation has its challenges.

Possibly the best situation for a new leader is one in which he or she is in the same organization, but a different section or department. Assigning newly promoted people in this manner is common in many organizations. Usually, these leaders at least know the people who will be their followers, but may not have fully developed working relationships with them. Consequently, they have less "old baggage" to overcome and can concentrate on leadership tasks and functions without old habits getting in the way.

Regardless of the situation in which you become a leader, start your leadership career properly. You will find it easier to develop the right habits and practices with a clean slate than to have to change bad habits later. That is not to say that you should expect to perform perfectly from the beginning. Leadership, like any other career, requires practice and development. Your skills improve over time, hopefully, just as in any other career. Continually striving to improve your leadership skills and abilities, and understanding they will never be perfect are critical to your success as a leader. Many resources exist to help you in this ongoing development.

Try reading at least a few of the literally thousands of books available on the topic of leadership. Even if you read one, with which you do not agree, you have gained something valuable! Keep in mind that the writers of all those books – including me and this book – have their own opinions about leadership. Accept the fact that you are as smart as they are and use your own good judgment to assess and weigh what they have written. You might have a better idea! Just as suggestions, I have listed some of my favorite written leadership resources as an appendix to this book.

Find a mentor. Think of someone in your past or present whom you regard as a good leader, then copy his or her leadership behaviors. If possible, ask that person to be a mentor and have regular coaching/mentoring sessions to discuss leadership. Go to these sessions armed with situations you have faced, both successes and failures, and discuss why your techniques for handling those situations worked or failed to work. Understand that you will not be successful every time. Use your failures to learn as much as you do from successful challenges – they are often more revealing.

Attend leadership training sessions or seminars. Again, any such training is useful, even if you disagree with what the presenter/instructor says. Unfortunately, one of the most prevalent mistakes I have observed in organizations is promoting individuals into leadership roles and giving them no opportunity to learn the new skills required to be successful. If necessary, request such training. Successful leaders tend not to shy away from asking for what they need. Keep in mind that the second major function of leadership addressed in chapter one involves providing people the resources they need to be successful. Resources include training and the acquisition of new skills. Your leader, however, may not realize you need to gain these skills, so ask!

Learn to observe human behavior and understand human nature. Allow people to be people first and then employees or volunteers. Empathize with them. Help them develop by jointly setting high standards and goals, then assisting them in reaching them. Establishing clear expectations "up front" ensures people know what you expect from them. Remember, your first function as a leader is to provide guidance and vision. The most common mistake I have seen leaders make, especially new leaders, is failing to provide clear expectations. Generally, people want to perform the tasks for which they are responsible successfully and well. Not knowing what those tasks are puts them at a distinct disadvantage. Unfortunately, many leaders expect people to gain this knowledge through osmosis.

Be willing to put your own desires and preferences aside occasionally in order to allow others to follow theirs, even if doing so means making a small mistake – people often learn best through making mistakes. Solve problems together, soliciting and using others' input and allow people to try things on their own sometimes. Sure, they may fail or make a mistake, but they will learn valuable lessons in problem solving through doing so.

Example

Did you ever learn to ride a bicycle? Most people did. Has it been a considerable time since you last rode one? Even if it has been many years, chances are good that if presented with the opportunity, you could still ride a bicycle. You might be a little shaky at first, but you could do it.

Now, did you initially learn to ride a bicycle without falling off a couple times? Probably not. Most of us, in fact, do fall a few times while learning to ride. Once we learn the balance and timing, however, we have it for life. Without practicing this set of skills for many years, we retain the basic knowledge and ability to perform the task of riding a bicycle. I maintain that falling off a few times helps people learn these skills.

Above all else, when you become a leader remember what it was like to be a follower. Most people declare at some point that things would be or will be different if and when they are in charge. Then they receive a promotion and seem to forget what it was like on the receiving end of bad leadership. If necessary, spend some time "in the trenches" to re-acquaint yourself with the conditions, stresses, and expectations at that level. Get feedback from your followers on how you are doing as a leader. Considering that some of them will feel uncomfortable providing that feedback, you may need to develop anonymous methods to gather the information.

The main point here is to take your leadership responsibilities seriously and keep followers in mind.

Remember that you cannot get everything done yourself – you *need* these people! Providing them with the information and resources they need to do whatever job or task you have asked them do only makes sense. Your leadership tasks can be relatively easy or difficult. It all depends on how you approach them.

Now go out and lead someone.

Chapter Seven
Leadership Lessons I've Learned

Never pass up a chance to learn something new about leadership in general or about your leadership style specifically. You will learn many of these lessons the hard way, unfortunately, by making a poor decision or choice, thus resulting in consequences other than those you intend. You will also learn many by making good decisions and choices, hopefully resulting in the intended consequences. In either case, reflecting on your leadership behaviors occasionally helps you distill the myriad actions you take as a leader into clear, definable actions that will serve you well over the years.

This chapter presents some of the lessons I have learned since getting into the leadership business. Some are from life, in general, and some are from more specific leadership situations. In each case, I have included the story of how I learned that particular lesson. If any of them sound familiar – and I suspect some will – rest assured you are developing as a leader in much the same way as everyone has throughout the history of leadership.

You may want to keep a leadership journal to jot down your leadership lessons. It doesn't matter if you are a brand new leader or if you have been in the business 50 years – we never stop learning to be better leaders. Such a journal helps you remember these little gems and makes for very enlightening reading now and then. Looking back over your notes occasionally reminds you of those lessons and helps you to remember to follow them.

Lesson: *It's not what you say, it's how you say it.*

I cannot begin to tell you how incredibly tired I got of hearing my father say this. Mind you, I was a good kid, relatively speaking. My older brother got in enough trouble for both of us. Yet any time one of us would come off with a little attitude, we heard this line. Dad was not known for his tolerance of teenage attitude.

Now, keep in mind that we cannot see attitude. We see only the behaviors associated with the attitude. Communication is extremely complex. We communicate incredible amounts of information with the slightest of actions – verbal tone and inflection, our choice of specific words, facial expressions, body posture, rolling the eyes, etc. So what my dad was really saying was that he could see through what I was saying and receive my true meaning by the vast majority of my communication behaviors – my attitude.

Others react the same way. Telling someone what we want him or her to do is effective only when it is said in the appropriate manner. People will see through the spoken word and understand when you are putting them down or when you do not believe in the guidance yourself. Make sure your communications are sincere and genuine. Otherwise, you may get results other than those you intend.

Source of the lesson: H. R. "Mickie" Corkran, my dad

Lesson: *People need praise.*

Probably the first lesson I ever learned in my military training came during my sophomore year in high school Junior ROTC, and I have always remembered it. Our Senior Army Instructor (SAI) was teaching the class that day. I remember that he seemed so old to me – then. (He was probably in his mid- to late-40s at the time.) He stated that soldiers need three things: food, to include water; shelter, to include clothing and protection from the elements; and a pat on the back for doing a good job. He went on to say that this applied to all people, because that's all soldiers are – normal people. That made me think about my own motivation for accomplishing tasks or actions. He was right – I much preferred positive reinforcement to punishment. Of course, I did not understand positive reinforcement theory at the time, but I did understand recognition for something well done.

Punishment certainly has its place. We cannot ignore poor performance, nor should we. Our first tactic, however, should be to encourage excellent performance through appropriate development and recognition. I believe that people want to do what is right and perform well, and that providing frequent appropriate pats on the back is the way to get them to perform to the high standards we set.

Source of the lesson: LTC (Ret.) M. M. DePass, Senior Army Instructor, Dothan High School

My first assignment in the Army was in 1st Battalion, 32nd Armor, within the 3rd Armored Division, first as a platoon leader in Company A, then as the Executive Officer of Headquarters Company. This assignment was the source of many of my best-learned leadership lessons. A little like learning to ride a bicycle, learning to lead often involves falling down a lot by making the wrong choices or decisions. Hopefully, those wrong choices do not cause serious problems, but sometimes they do. The next few lessons are ones I learned while in that assignment.

Lesson: *Excuses don't work – even when you are right.*

As a young lieutenant, "additional duties" often comprised as much of my workload as my primary duties. As the Supply Officer for my company, I spent a great deal of time and effort in the supply room, often trying to figure things out as much as doing anything proactive. When the division instituted a new supply and maintenance inspection program, the Supply Sergeant and I spent many hours to ensure all the supplies and equipment, as well as their accompanying paperwork, was ready for our turn in the inspection cycle.

As expected, we finally got the call that we would be inspected. We failed miserably, in both the first and second inspections. As much as we tried, we could not reach the standard required to pass the inspection. Our Supply Room was in good shape – as good as anyone's and better than most – but we just could not seem to reach the standard, which I thought was unrealistic. I explained my concern regarding the standard to my commander, Captain Ed Dyer, who is the source of this lesson.

Captain Dyer agreed with me that the standards were unrealistically high, requiring virtual perfection. He further stated that complaining about the standards would be perceived by the command as an excuse for failure, something none of us wanted. He explained to me that we had to pass the inspection first, and then voice our concerns that the standards were too high, requiring far more time and effort than the situation warranted.

As I recall, we never "passed" the inspection, though CPT Dyer and the entire company were recognized later as having achieved the highest score in the division. We spent a great deal of time and effort to achieve the level we did and it had little to do with our ability to perform our primary mission, but we achieved it nonetheless. I do not remember if the standards were made more realistic, but I do know that I learned a lesson from it.

Source of the lesson: Captain Edward L. Dyer, Commander, Company A, 1st Battalion, 32nd Armor. (Incidentally, CPT Dyer later retired as a Brigadier General, and remains one of the leaders I have met whom I most admire.)

Lesson: *Set high standards and see them through.*

My unit in Germany was scheduled to conduct a road march (convoy) of 150 – 200 miles on January 1, 1979. The day before, we got a bad ice storm that made all the roads in the area extremely treacherous. A road march of that length, at that point in time, was dangerous enough under good conditions. Driving 100 or more military vehicles so far usually meant breakdowns and possibly an accident. Considering safety, we knew the road march would be postponed, allowing us to spend New Year's Day with our families. We were wrong. Nothing was canceled, nothing was postponed. The road march went as scheduled, with added emphasis on the safety aspects.

The Battalion Commander's point was that the enemy would not necessarily attack in good weather, and we needed to be prepared to go to war at any time, in any weather. (Remember, this was during the Cold War – no pun intended.) During our final briefings, he stressed how careful we had to be and how treacherous the road conditions were. For the road march, I was serving as a "stick leader," guiding 10 – 12 jeeps and trucks.

The trip took what seemed to be an intolerable time, during which I had to relieve my driver for a few hours because he was getting sleepy. The drivers of the vehicles following me, almost all without radios or other communication, followed faithfully but at safe distances. The trip took almost 12 hours, but we all made it – tired but safe, with no accidents or mishaps. In fact, the entire battalion's wheeled vehicles made it with no accidents that I remember.

Through the experience, we all learned that we could make such a move in virtually any weather and without any real problems. It was hard, but we accomplished the mission.

Source of the lesson: Lieutenant Colonel Larry Beale, who was then Commander, 1st Battalion 32nd Armor.

Lesson: *Integrity is non-negotiable.*

One beautiful weekend – a relatively rare event in central Europe – I was on call for the company if an officer was needed. As such, I was to stay at home close to the phone. In a moment of nothing less than stupidity, I allowed myself to be talked into going for a "short" drive in the country. We were gone only a couple hours and I had never known an officer to be called on the weekend. This weekend was different.

During the time I was away from the phone, a fight broke out in the barracks and a soldier was badly hurt. Because I was not where I should have been, the NCO in charge of the barracks for the day could not reach me. Obviously, my commander wanted to know why I had been out of contact. I had no excuse, of course. I had let my integrity fail and done something other than what I should have been doing.

My commander was as forgiving as commanders can be in such situations, though he did have to take some minor actions against me. I survived that incident and never let my integrity falter in that way again.

Source of the lesson: My commander in HHC, 1-32 Armor. Sorry, I have forgotten his name, but not the incident.

Lesson: *Sometimes you have to take responsibility for something you did not do.*

Within our local training area, we had a facility called the Mini Tank Range. It was a relatively small facility where we could practice tank gunnery techniques using frangible 7.62 mm ammunition in our tanks' coaxial machine guns. (Don't worry if you do not understand the terms here – they are irrelevant to the lesson.)

One day, my platoon was on the Mini Tank Range conducting gunnery training. As the Officer-in-Charge/Safety Officer, I was responsible for ensuring the safety of everyone on the range. The 7.62 mm rounds were frangible, meaning they would disintegrate upon hitting the concrete and steel back of the range, but they were still deadly to people. Consequently, one of my duties was to clear each weapon before anyone went downrange to change targets or conduct maintenance. Prior to moving down range, I cleared all machine guns on the firing line. To this day, I am absolutely sure I physically inspected each gun. Nonetheless, while we were down range, one gun went off, sending a bullet into our area. Fortunately, no one was hurt, but it should not have happened.

When discussing this with me, the Battalion Commander honestly believed that I had cleared the gun. The incident was, however, a serious safety violation that I could not explain and for which he had to take negative action – a letter of reprimand. Consequently, I accepted the responsibility for what had happened. It was the right thing to do. In further training on the range, however, I took additional steps to prevent such an incident recurring.

Source of the lesson: Lieutenant Colonel Ronald Griffith, Commander, 1st Battalion 32nd Armor. (LTC Griffith was later GEN Ronald Griffith, Vice Chief of Staff, U.S. Army.)

Lesson: *People who never make mistakes never do anything at all.*

During an extended training exercise, my platoon was "out in the boonies." In those situations, soldiers really appreciate a hot meal after eating "C" rations for a few days. (Now they eat Meals, Ready to Eat – MREs. This was during the late 1970s.) One evening, the battalion had scheduled a hot meal for supper. As was usually the case, an NCO would deliver the meal to our location. In this case, that NCO was not from my company, but was someone assigned from headquarters to deliver the meal.

Our soldiers had been subsisting on C rations for a few days, so they were enthusiastic about receiving the hot "chow." Supper time came and went and no food arrived.

Each radio call to headquarters assured me it was on its way. Supper finally arrived – at 3:00 a.m. Naturally, I was a bit upset with the NCO delivering the meal. He very calmly listened to what I had to say, apologized profusely for the delay, and explained he had gotten "temporarily misoriented" – Army-speak for lost. After a few more choice words from me, he smiled genuinely and said, "Lieutenant, you show me a man who never makes a mistake, and I'll show you someone who doesn't do a damn thing." I could not stop myself from chuckling and thanking him for his persistence in getting to us.

In spite of the hour, the soldiers enjoyed the food that was no longer very hot. Over the next few days, this NCO made sure to get our hot meals to us on time, often putting us first for delivery. Each time he came to our site, I thanked him for being prompt and we had a chuckle about the first time.

Source of the lesson: Unfortunately, I no longer remember this sergeant's name, but I have never forgotten the lesson.

There are many more lessons I learned while in that assignment, but I will save them for later.

Lesson: *We cannot always achieve the desired goal.*

Nearly all organizations – military or civilian, business or non-profit, government or private sector – strive for perfection. We set high standards and expect people to reach them. Setting high standards is good and necessary, providing they can be reached.

From 1986 to 1990, I was assigned as the Chief of the Armor and Infantry Team at Readiness Group Knox, part of the 2nd U.S. Army. Our mission was to provide training and technical assistance to units of the U. S. Army Reserve and the Kentucky National Guard. Filled with extremely dedicated and committed individuals, these units frequently called on the team for help. In nearly every case, the results were excellent and these units and personnel were just one step closer to being prepared to go to war should the need arise. In some cases, however, our efforts seemed to have little to no effect.

In one of these situations, I became very frustrated when our training and assistance just did not seem to be sinking in. My very professional and understanding team of expert NCOs worked hard to help a particular unit improve, without ever reaching the standard. Certainly they improved, but failed to meet the rather high standard set by the Army. Venting my frustration to my commander one day, he told me, "Jeff, sometimes good enough is good enough. Has the unit improved?"

"Yes, sir," I replied.

"Then you have accomplished something. Why are you so frustrated?" the Colonel asked.

"The unit can meet the standard, sir. I'm sure of it," I said, "A few individuals, including their commander, are getting in the way of reaching the goal."

After hearing me out, Colonel Keivit patted my back and assured me I was doing alright. He then counseled me to keep at it and understand that it would take longer than initially expected.

Source of the lesson: COL Bob Keivit, Commander, Readiness Group Knox

Lesson: *As leaders, we never stop learning.*

After retiring from the Army, I went to work as a trainer and training consultant with the Center for Quality Training at Elizabethtown Community College in Kentucky.

My boss, Beth, was relatively new in her job as Director of the center, though she had worked as the Continuing Education Coordinator for several years. Now she was faced with having to lead the department, primarily consisting of people with whom she had worked for several years in a different capacity. Two of us, however, were a little out of the ordinary for the office: Lindon, a woman who had owned several of her own businesses, and me, a retired Army officer. As you might expect, we were both a little headstrong and sure we could make all necessary decisions.

Early in my tenure with the college, Lindon, Beth and I butted heads numerous times, creating considerable tension. Through the next few years, the rift between Beth and Lindon became wider and Lindon left the organization. I, however, was determined to work through the problems and differences and stay. Beth and I spoke several times about the situation and agreed to try hard to work together to reach a better level of understanding. She said she knew that neither of us was perfect but that she would really appreciate my help in leading the organization to new levels.

For the remainder of the 10 years we worked together, Beth and I got along very well, weathering the occasional disagreement well. She changed dramatically, continually

109

learning and challenging herself to improve her own skills, while encouraging the rest of us to do the same. The result was a solid team, capable of handling any crisis or challenge presented to us with skill, humor, and style. When the Community College and the Technical College merged, we were the first office to co-locate and become one, all of which we accomplished with no major problems, thanks primarily to Beth's leadership and her support of the people in the organization.

Source of the lesson: Ms. Beth Nickell, Director, Community and Economic Development Center, Elizabethtown Community and Technical College.

Having spent over 30 years in various capacities within the leadership business, I have certainly learned many more lessons – some concerning things I have done right and others concerning actions I took that had abysmal results. You, too, will experience success and failure along your leadership journey. The key, of course, is to learn from each experience, whether good or bad.

As you lead others, just remember to see the road from their perspective. Make sure they know where you want them to go. Take the time and make the effort to ensure they have everything they need to accomplish goals and try to help them enjoy the journey as much as you do. Steering the wheel will help you do these things smoothly and effectively.

Bibliography and Suggested Reading

Blanchard, Kenneth and Johnson, Spencer, *The One-Minute Manager*, New York: Blanchard Family Partnership and Candle Communications Corporation, 1981.

Collins, Jim, *Good to Great: Why Some Companies Make the Leap and Others Don't*, New York: HarperCollins Publishers Inc., 2001.

Metcalf, C.W. and Felible, Roma, *Lighten Up: Survival Skills for People under Pressure*, New York: Basic Books, 1998.

Miller, Susan, *Oomph Power!: How to Get Re-Energized for Outrageous Success*, Prospect, KY: Simpson*Wesley Publishers, 2003.

Ziglar, Zig, with Dhanam, Krish; Flanagan, Bryan; and Savage, Jim, *Top Performance: How to Develop Excellence in Yourself and Others*, Grand Rapids: Revell, 2004.

Contact Information

To contact Jeff:
- C2C Training and Consulting, 108 Amanda Court, Radcliff, KY 40160
- www.c2ctrainers.com
- jeff@c2ctrainers.com
- 270-317-3090